Your Relationship Report Card

∽∽♡♡∽

Gregory J.P. Godek

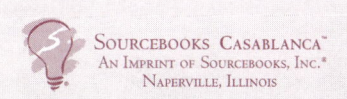

SOURCEBOOKS CASABLANCA™
AN IMPRINT OF SOURCEBOOKS, INC.®
NAPERVILLE, ILLINOIS

Copyright © 2007 by Gregory J.P. Godek
Cover and internal design © 2007 by
Sourcebooks, Inc.
Sourcebooks and the colophon are registered
trademarks of Sourcebooks, Inc.

All rights reserved. No part of this book may be reproduced in any form or by any electronic or mechanical means including information storage and retrieval systems—except in the case of brief quotations embodied in critical articles or reviews—without permission in writing from its publisher, Sourcebooks, Inc.

Published by Sourcebooks, Inc.
P.O. Box 4410, Naperville, Illinois 60567-4410
(630) 961-3900
Fax: (630) 961-2168
www.sourcebooks.com

ISBN-13: 978-1-4022-0893-5
ISBN-10: 1-4022-0893-6

Printed and bound in Canada
WC 10 9 8 7 6 5 4 3 2 1

Your Relationship Report Card allows you to grade yourself and your partner on a number of skills that contribute to a successful love relationship. By comparing how you both act in your relationship, you will gain insights into the dynamics of yourselves as a unique couple.

Remember, getting straight A's is *not* the goal! We all have strengths and weaknesses. The goal is to raise your awareness, help you appreciate strengths, and shed some light on areas that aren't working as well as they could be.

Each of you grades yourself and your partner in key relationship skills. It's best if Partner #2 covers up the column with Partner #1's answers. Below are some basics; the following pages introduce some expanded topics and scenarios to get you thinking. When you're both done, share the results. Have fun!

- **A** = Passionate, exciting, fulfilling—not perfect, but clearly excellent

- **B** = Very good—solid, better-than-most, consistent, improving

- **C** = Average—adequate, acceptable, okay, static

- **D** = Below average—not good, but not hopeless

- **F** = Hopeless, dismal, unhappy—definitely not working

Relationship Skills

Partner 1 — Me/You   **Partner 2** — Me/You

Partner 1		Partner 2
___/___	Attitude	___/___
___/___	Commitment	___/___
___/___	Considerateness	___/___
___/___	Couple-thinking	___/___
___/___	Flexibility	___/___
___/___	Playfulness	___/___
___/___	Responsibility	___/___
___/___	Romance	___/___
___/___	Sense of humor	___/___
___/___	Sensitivity	___/___
___/___	Spontaneity	___/___
___/___	Trust	___/___

Partner 1 — Me/You

Affection

Partner 2 — Me/You

___/___ 1. How well do you think you express affection? How well does your partner express affection? (Grade from A+ to F)   ___/___

___/___ 2. What is your style of showing affection? Your partner's?
    a. Verbal, friendly
    b. Quirky, creative
    c. Physical, sensuous
    d. Courteous, classical   ___/___

___/___ 3. What sorts of gifts do you normally give to your partner? Your partner to you?
    a. Flowers/candy
    b. Gag gifts
    c. Jewelry
    d. Surprise outings   ___/___

___/___ 4. What do you typically do to show affection? Your partner?
    a. Say "I love you"
    b. A humorous greeting card
    c. A call from work
    d. A kiss   ___/___

<table>
<tr><td>Partner 1
Me/You</td><td># Arguing Skills</td><td>Partner 2
Me/You</td></tr>
</table>

___/___ 1. Rate your ability to forgive your partner after a fight (from A+ to F). Your partner's?   ___/___

___/___ 2. Rate your anger level on a scale of 1–10 during a fight. Your partner's?   ___/___

___/___ 3. What sort of issues anger you the most? Your partner?   ___/___
  a. Money
  b. Romance (or lack thereof)
  c. Sex (or lack thereof)
  d. Issues with immediate and/or extended family

___/___ 4. How do you cope with your anger during a fight? Your partner?   ___/___
  a. Taking a five-minute break to collect yourself
  b. Storming away and slamming the bedroom door behind you
  c. Name-calling or threatening
  d. Other _____

Communication

Partner 1 Me/You **Partner 2** Me/You

___/___ 1. Grade your communication skills (from A+ to F). Your partner's? ___/___

___/___ 2. Which of the following best describes your communication style? Your partner's? ___/___
   a. Open and honest
   b. Withdrawn
   c. Talkative, chatty
   d. Sarcastic or defensive

___/___ 3. You are feeling upset about a comment your partner made in passing yesterday. What do you do? What would your partner do? ___/___
   a. Stew silently, but never mention it
   b. Berate your partner about it the first time he/she irritates you
   c. Sit down with him/her and discuss why the comment hurt your feelings

continued...

| Partner 1 Me/You | Communication | Partner 2 Me/You |

___/___ 4. There is an expensive item that you would love to receive as a present. However, the price tag is a bit steep, and you don't want to put pressure on your lover to overspend. What do you do? Your partner? ___/___
  a. Hint to your partner that you really like this particular item
  b. Tell your partner directly that you would like this as a gift
  c. Keep quiet about it, but feel wistful when the holiday passes

Partner 1 — Me/You

Compromise

Partner 2 — Me/You

___/___ 1. Grade your overall ability to compromise (during arguments, financial planning, event planning, parenting, etc.) (from A+ to F). Your partner?   ___/___

___/___ 2. On a whim, you buy tickets to see your favorite singer (whom your partner dislikes). Too late, you realize that the concert falls on your partner's birthday. What do you do? What would your partner do?   ___/___
   a. Tell your partner "too bad"—this performer rarely ever comes to town
   b. Give the tickets to someone else and chalk it up to an impulse buy
   c. Plan something special for your partner to do while you are at the concert
   d. Leave it up to your partner and gladly do what they choose

continued...

Compromise

Partner 1 Me/You ___/___

Partner 2 Me/You ___/___

3. You are car shopping and find the car of your dreams, however, it is several thousand dollars out of your price range. You want the car, but your partner insists you buy a cheaper model. What do you do? What would your partner do in the same situation?
    a. Agree that the car is too expensive and continue your search
    b. Promise that you will cut your spending to make up for the steep price tag
    c. Insist on this car and refuse to take "no" for an answer
    d. Negotiate a scenario that will satisfy you both

Creativity

Partner 1 — Me/You   *Partner 2 — Me/You*

___/___ 1. How creative are you when it comes to love and romance (from A+ to F)? Your partner?   ___/___

___/___ 2. What is the biggest impediment to your creativity? Your partner?
   a. Not enough time or money
   b. Fear of failure and/or embarrassment
   c. Believing that you're not creative
   d. Stress or fatigue   ___/___

___/___ 3. Which of the following describes you best? Your partner?
   a. A playful attitude
   b. Willingness to take risks
   c. Believing that you are creative
   d. A humorous approach to romance   ___/___

___/___ 4. How would it be easiest for you to start expanding your romantic creativity? For your partner?
   a. Initiating more and different plans or outings
   b. Buying more thoughtful, meaningful gifts
   c. Spicing up your sex life with new techniques or accessories
   d. Other _____   ___/___

Financial Responsibility

Partner 1 — Me/You
Partner 2 — Me/You

___/___ 1. Grade your level of financial responsibility (from A+ to F). Your partner's? ___/___

___/___ 2. What best describes your spending style? Your partner's? ___/___
   a. Budget-conscious
   b. Impulse spender
   c. Charge now, pay later
   d. Generous to a fault

___/___ 3. The monthly bills come in. How do you deal with them? Your partner? ___/___
   a. Let them accumulate on the counter until the day before they're due
   b. Pay them immediately as they arrive
   c. Forget about them until after they're due
   d. Set up online "auto-pay" accounts so that you will never forget

continued...

Financial Responsibility

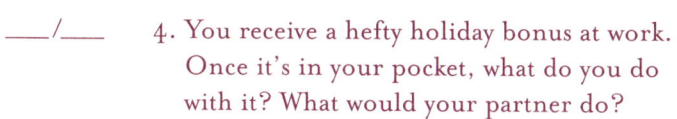

Partner 1 Me/You   ___/___

Partner 2 Me/You   ___/___

4. You receive a hefty holiday bonus at work. Once it's in your pocket, what do you do with it? What would your partner do?
   a. Spend it on something you need around the house (e.g., appliances, furniture, etc.)
   b. Go on a shopping spree in the most expensive shops in town
   c. Invest it in a mutual fund, stock, or retirement account
   d. Put it into your checking or savings account

Friendship

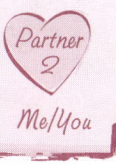

Partner 1 — Me/You *Partner 2 — Me/You*

___/___ 1. Grade the quality of friendship you provide your partner (from A+ to F), as well as the quality of friendship your partner provides you.

___/___ 2. Who knows you the best? Who knows your partner the best?
   a. Partner—you two are best friends
   b. Family member (parent, sibling, cousin, etc.)
   c. Best friend

___/___ 3. What is your favorite fun, non-sexual activity? Your partner's?
   a. Snuggling up in pajamas and watching a movie
   b. Going out to eat at a favorite restaurant
   c. Going for a walk or hike
   d. Other _____

___/___ 4. What is the one thing you would find most difficult to forgive, in any friendship? Your partner?
   a. Infidelity
   b. Verbal abuse
   c. Physical abuse
   d. Dishonesty

<table>
<tr><th>Partner 1
Me/You</th><th align="center"># Generosity</th><th>Partner 2
Me/You</th></tr>
<tr><td>___/___</td><td>1. Grade how generous you and your partner are (from A+ to F).</td><td>___/___</td></tr>
<tr><td>___/___</td><td>2. A disheveled-looking man is sitting on the sidewalk with a sign begging for money. What do you do? What would your partner do?
  a. Empty your wallet into his hands
  b. Give him some loose change
  c. Pass him without making eye contact</td><td>___/___</td></tr>
<tr><td>___/___</td><td>3. Your sister is getting married. What do you give as a gift? What would your partner give?
  a. A card with money inside
  b. A household appliance or accessory that she needs
  c. Something personalized that will remind her of the special bond you share
  d. Other _____</td><td>___/___</td></tr>
<tr><td>___/___</td><td>4. How often do you buy gifts for your partner? How often does he/she buy them for you?
  a. Often—once a week or more
  b. Occasionally—every few weeks
  c. Only on holidays
  d. Never</td><td>___/___</td></tr>
</table>

Partner 1 — Me/You

Honesty

Partner 2 — Me/You

___/___ 1. Grade how honest you are with your partner (from A+ to F). How honest do you think your partner is with you? ___/___

___/___ 2. Your ex is in town and wants to take you to dinner to catch up. What do you do? What would your partner do? ___/___
   a. Politely decline the offer and neglect to mention it to your partner
   b. Tell your partner that you're going to dinner with a friend (without specifying who)
   c. Discuss it with your partner—he/she deserves to know about it, whether or not you accept the invitation

continued...

Honesty

Partner 1 — Me/You

Partner 2 — Me/You

___/___ 3. Against your better judgment, you purchase an expensive item that you've been eyeing for months, even though finances are tight. What would you do? Your partner? ___/___
   a. Confess to your partner that you caved in and offer to cut back on your spending to pay it off
   b. Charge it to a credit card that your partner doesn't know about and hide the item
   c. Wait until your partner notices the item, and then lie about the price

___/___ 4. Your partner cooks you a surprise dinner. You take a bite and the food is awful. How would you react? Your partner? ___/___
   a. Gush about how wonderful the meal is to show your appreciation
   b. Wait for your partner's reaction to the food—if he/she looks disgusted, share your honest opinion
   c. Comment immediately that you think the food is awful

Household Management

Partner 1 Me/You

Partner 2 Me/You

___/___ 1. How would you grade your household management skills (from A+ to F)? Your partner's?   ___/___

___/___ 2. What is your greatest strength in managing your home? Your partner's?   ___/___
    a. Finances
    b. Cleaning/organizing
    c. Doing yard work
    d. Doing the errands

___/___ 3. What is your greatest weakness in managing your home? Your partner's?   ___/___
    a. Finances
    b. Cleaning/organizing
    c. Doing yard work
    d. Doing the errands

___/___ 4. What is your biggest pet peeve around the house? Your partner's?   ___/___
    a. Dirty dishes
    b. Piles of unsorted mail
    c. Unmown grass
    d. Other _____

Partner 1		Partner 2
Me/You	# Listening Skills	Me/You

___/___ 1. How good a listener are you? Your partner? (Grade from A+ to F)   ___/___

___/___ 2. A *passive listener* is someone who listens to what his/her partner is saying, but is thinking in terms of himself/herself. An *active listener* listens with *empathy* (stepping into his/her partner's shoes). What do you consider yourself to be most often? Your partner?
   a. Passive listener
   b. Active listener

___/___ 3. When you and your partner are having a discussion, do you usually find yourself: ___/___
   a. Interrupting
   b. Listening intently
   c. Tuning him/her out
   d. Dredging up past disagreements

___/___ 4. What is most important to you during an argument or discussion?   ___/___
   a. Empathy
   b. Not being judged
   c. Reassurance
   d. Finding solutions to problems

<table>
<tr><td>Partner 1
Me/You</td><td style="text-align:center"># Lovemaking</td><td>Partner 2
Me/You</td></tr>
</table>

___/___ 1. Grade your libido over the course of the last month (from A+ to F). Your partner's libido?   ___/___

___/___ 2. What is your favorite type of kiss? Your partner's?   ___/___
   a. Light and delicate
   b. Hard and fast
   c. Soft, slow, and sensuous
   d. Deep and wet

___/___ 3. Where do you fantasize about making love, but have never done it? Where do you think your partner would like to make love?   ___/___
   a. In the backseat of a car or limousine
   b. In an elevator
   c. In your partner's office, on the desk
   d. Other _____

___/___ 4. Which type of lovemaking do you prefer? Your partner?   ___/___
   a. Planned, slow, and quiet
   b. Spontaneous, fast, and loud
   c. Traditional and comforting
   d. Naughty and daring

| Partner 1 Me/You | # Patience | Partner 2 Me/You |

___/___ 1. How patient are you (grade from A+ to F)? ___/___
How patient is your partner?

___/___ 2. Your partner is shopping for new clothes ___/___
and has asked you to stick around while
he/she tries things on. You look at your
watch and realize that three hours have
passed and he/she hasn't liked a single
outfit. What do you do? What would your
partner do?
   a. Grow impatient and start tapping your foot or giving your partner pointed looks
   b. Put your best face forward—after all, your partner often indulges you
   c. Snap at your partner and tell him/her to call your cell phone when he/she is done

continued...

Partner 1 Me/You

Patience

Partner 2 Me/You

___/___ 3. Your partner bought a top-secret gift for you and ordered you not to peek. You know where it is hidden. Would you/your partner: ___/___
   a. Peek anyway—patience isn't your strong suit
   b. Respect your partner's wishes and steer clear of the gift

___/___ 4. Your partner is half an hour late coming home from work after promising to help you around the house. Would you/your partner: ___/___
   a. Get frustrated and start the housework on your own
   b. Call your partner to express concern
   c. Call your partner to nag him/her
   d. Pour yourself a glass of wine and wait patiently—he/she must be caught in traffic

Partner 1 Me/You|	|Partner 2 Me/You

___/___   1. How would you grade your self-esteem (from A+ to F)? Your partner's?   ___/___

___/___   2. In which area do you feel *most* confident? Your partner?   ___/___
         a. Your worth as a lover
         b. Your career-related abilities
         c. Special talents (writing, singing, athleticism, etc.)
         d. Other _____

___/___   3. In which area do you feel *least* confident? Your partner?   ___/___
         a. Your worth as a lover
         b. Your career-related abilities
         c. Special talents (writing, singing, athleticism, etc.)
         d. Other _____

continued...

Self-esteem

___/___ 4. What might you do to boost your partner's self-esteem? What might your partner do to boost yours?   ___/___
   a. Take them out for dinner in celebration of an accomplishment
   b. Make a list of your ten (or more) favorite things about your partner
   c. More encouragement and understanding
   d. More compliments and less criticism

Also by Gregory J.P. Godek

1001 Ways to Be Romantic

10,000 Ways to Say I Love You

Love Coupons

I Love You Coupons